God is in control

CARMEN BARTON

Ordering Information:

Prime Seven Media
518 Landmann St.
Tomah City, WI 54660

Printed in the United States of America

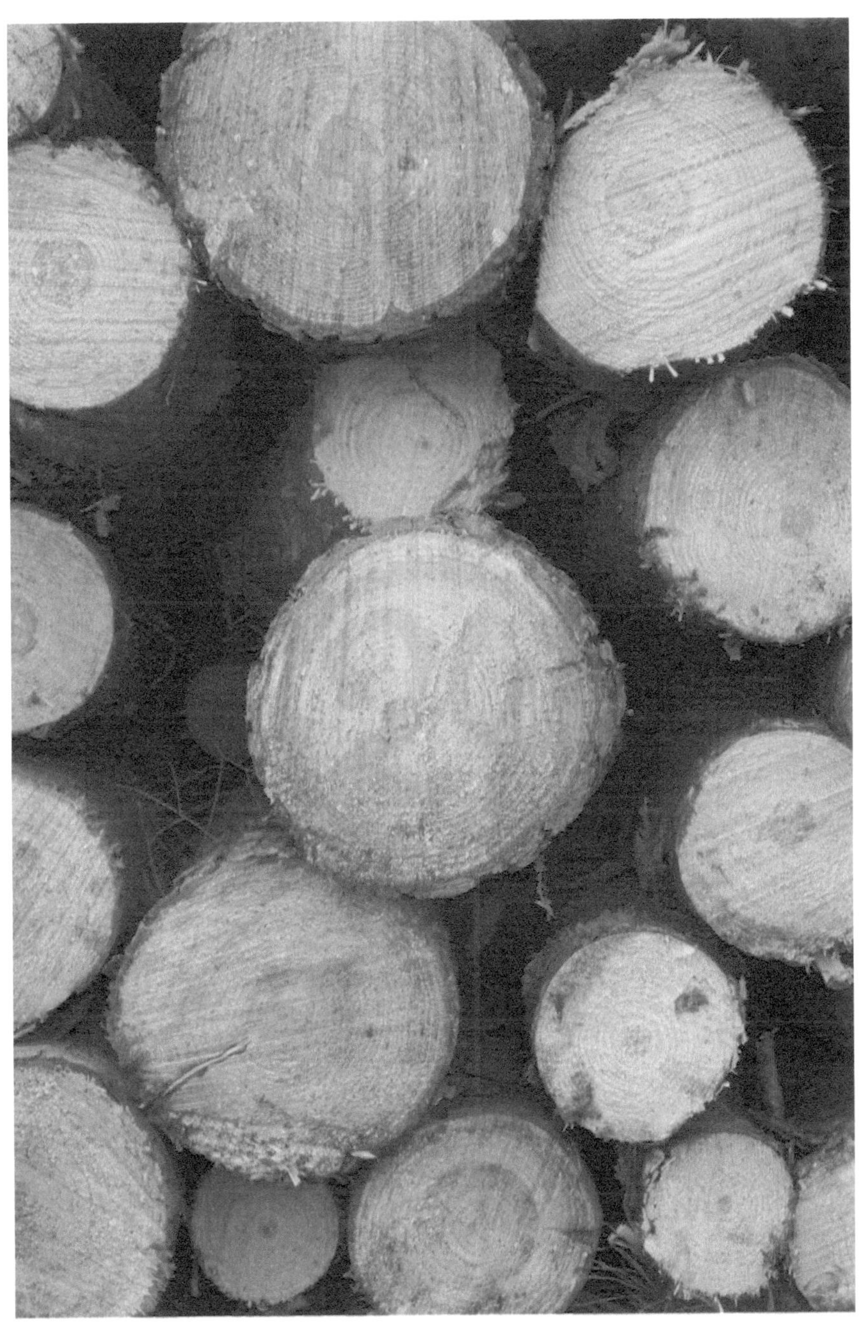

Table of Contents

Preface

The family I grew up in had incompatible characters, probably because we were partly only half related, and some of us were so different that we didn't get along well, which resulted in a lot of misery, at a certain point I just felt running away as quickly as possible. To top it all off, I was also misdiagnosed because of their lies. And not only that, they also managed to release a book about me, without my knowledge, based on stolen medical files and a diary that someone kept about me, how criminal. I will explain here how that could have happened.

With this book I show that God is judging, it is too late to repent now, of course we must forgive each other for the mistakes we make, we are all human. Forgiveness also for yourself, God's ways are unfathomable, whoever digs a pit for someone else will sooner or later ultimately falls into it themselves, if you do good things you will be rewarded, God represents the good: truth, purity, honesty, integrity, love and so on. Love for things and money is devilish and leads to nothing, it is the source of much misery, just like all other forms of lust.

It is very bad when people are unable to keep peace within their family, if that is not possible due to lack of compassion for each other or jealousy, how can you expect that there will be peace in the rest of the world, it is starting at a micro level, in everyday life.

In earlier times it was no different, Christ, to name just one name, broke with his family, he never spoke ill of them but had no further contact with them. Christ comes with the sword, it is described in the Bible, to judge and separate the wheat from the chaff. For many people this is probably hard to believe, they think that faith means being kind and friendly to everyone, at first glance this is true, however the Bible tells us to stay very far away from bad people.

And they exist, bad people.

You can hardly call someone who goes around murdering a good person. And there are people like that, those whom; in for example war situations would not turn their backs for one more or less human lives. Forgiveness is important, especially for yourself, to keep your heart pure.

However, forgiving someone does not mean that you have to continue the old way; a donkey does not hit the same stone three times. Forgive and choose a different path, without provoking a conflict or becoming involved in a conflict situation.

But my family is not exactly average, understatement! To begin with, my grandfather was married twice, which is not surprising, although I have absolutely no idea what caused his first wife, my grandmother, to die. Certain topics were kept silent within our family. As a child we learned that there were times when it was better not to ask questions. You learn to intuitively sense when silence is less risky. If only to protect yourself from yet another horror story that won't let you sleep at night.

His second wife came from the Veluwe, she grew up on a beautiful, very large, old mansion with a thatched roof, her father was Jewish and her mother perhaps too, it could be possible, she read a lot of books that is one of the few things I know about her. Her mothers name, Bolwiender, sounded quite German, although she was certainly not of German descent, just Dutch and her father's name was Meijer, it couldn't be more Jewish. Both his wives were of Jewish descent Hardly anyone from his first wife's family is still alive, it is a name that hardly occurs anymore, although her death has nothing to do with the Second World War, she had probably already died by then.

Her husband became a widower with no fewer than seven children, some of whom were still quite young at the time, and a number of them were placed here and there with family or friends. The eldest, Jan, possibly my biological father, ended up with monks when he was 12. Not fun either, he must have experienced it, especially when he was expected to become a priest; he was closer to crying than laughing. He also could hardly graduate from seminary; he wanted to date a girl, just like his peers, something he eventually managed to do.

That didn't happen without a fight; to begin with he even threw all his books into the ditch one day from the tower room of the castle where he lived. War broke out, he was ordained as a priest but had to go into hiding, immediately afterwards he left for South America and started working as a missionary in Brazil, which he continued for twenty years, a very difficult job. The task of a missionary was care and well-being, the Brazilians came to him for everything, they also saw him as a doctor, he was even called upon for deliveries. He had fulfilled his duties well and even went regularly sailing on a boat for three days across the Amazon, straight through the jungle to visit leper camps, very dangerous, it was in the sixties, when there was still really wild nature. A statue has been erected for him in Brazil.

Manaus, the capital of the Amazons, a province of Brazil, was still a very small village when he first arrived, he built a church there.

Grandfather had long since remarried and had nine more children, one of whom died, which was surrounded by the same mystery as the death of his first wife. Although there is something known about this girl that I am aware of, she became ill and was admitted to a sanatorium, exactly opposite the house where they used to live, I knew that there was a doctor, a sanatorium was new to me. A vague story, possibly it had something to do with the old sanatorium in Davos, my family, the Meijer's, already went on holiday in Switzerland when no one had ever heard of a holiday.

During the Second World War they were all wiped out, the number of deportees to Auschwitz with the surname Meijer was the largest group from The Netherlands, about thirty thousand, a black page in the history of our country and a big bite out of my family. If you search in archives you can come across all kinds of things. You can read how Jan fared in this book, a story in itself! Our family archive consisted of eight very thick, heavy, stuffed binders full of photos. I regularly visited an uncle, unfortunately deceased, who guarded the archive. Guarding, an appropriate term, the archive contained thousands of photos, a significant part of which was a hundred years old. The Meijer binder in particular was very valuable, most of the Meijer's of which there were still photos in the map were unable to tell the story of Auschwitz.

Introduction

The times we live in are not the easiest, contradictions seem greater than ever, Mother Earth is not happy either and God is watching, He is always in control. Although it does not seem that way and some people think differently. Following His Word is not always easy. Especially if the majority of humanity thinks differently, it is still important, as I explain in this book, and how you can apply this in daily life.

God represents all that is good, which is why many people think, "We have to help!" no matter what the issue is, they blindly follow leaders who may not have any good intentions at all. Political correctness plays a role in this, always wanting to be nice, often against all knowledge and also crossing boundaries. Countries often interfere too much with each other, not always in a positive way, every war is negative, and aggression must be banned.

I give examples from everyday life to illustrate this, and from my personal life. Moreover, this book is a manifesto for improvements, as a medical scientist I give you recommendations for what could be improved in healthcare, and how a person can become happy, perhaps the most important goal in life.

Due to his illness, Richard and I had to live separately for a while.

When at one point he had to be admitted for several months, this was the moment I finally got some rest after a lot of hectic activity.

One day I came across a painting that I had once bought at a thrift store in all my collecting frenzy, between jobs.

When I got home I put it down somewhere and didn't look at it seriously anymore due to lack of time, until that moment. I carefully picked it up from the corner where it stood and placed it on the table.

To properly study the back, I turned it over and placed it on a soft surface so as not to damage the front. Believe me, I had been working with the master painter, Richard Lee Barton, for twenty years at that time, and knew exactly how to handle precious paintings, although they certainly do not belong on the floor, so I immediately changed this after I had studied it for some time.

I discovered all kinds of things, there were all kinds of texts written on it: twenty guilders, the Old Dutch currency, would now have been about twenty dollars; a kind of street name; dimensions and so on.

It was an old handwriting and the cloth was also old.

"It can't be Van Gogh!" it suddenly occurred to me.

I did some research and sometime later came to the conclusion that it could well be possible, the colors red and green to start with were certainly his favorite colors and I discovered much more.

Years of research followed, especially in the area where I live, close to Nuenen. I also went back to the location where the painting was found, where I found three more works. First two works on canvas, later a watercolor on paper. With the knowledge I built up, I continued to search, on the one hand to prove its authenticity, and on the other hand to find even more works.

In fact, I had been looking for old paintings for a long time, hoping to one day find that one needle in a haystack. I had often come across all kinds of works by old masters.

In the past you did not have computers in which everything was registered, at least not in the time we are talking about here.

Selling art has always been a difficult profession, perhaps even more difficult than making art. Vincent van Gogh is a good example of this. During the Second World War, many collections were lost and works destroyed, so it goes without saying that the Nazis preferred not to have the papers there. Sometimes I think that the war was mainly about art, Hitler and Göring both wanted to start an art museum, separately, and had stored an enormous amount of art in underground corridors. They stole more than a few million works, they looted the whole of France and the Netherlands, and sometimes they even went to erase traces and did not hesitate to tinker with canvases. In this way, works ended up everywhere and nowhere. Vincent van Gogh's works may have played an important role in this because they were often not signed, which makes it more difficult to trace their origin.

For example, works by artists who often only had a real breakthrough after their death, great masters, can still be found in unexpected places. Research into the origin usually takes a lot of time. Owners of large collections are not always interested in such works; they want certainty, although they do not realize that even then things can go completely wrong or then just wrong.

People should start by restricting the making of reproductions, in all cases it should at least be clear that it is a reproduction, artists who commit plagiarism are, as far as I'm concerned, the worst thing there is and you can't actually be called artist. Whether it concerns writers or visual artists, in most cases a lot goes into it before you get to the point where a book or work of art is finished, such as study, research, investments, developing plans and so on. If someone just copies it one by one without even mentioning your name, it is very painful, actually a form of theft you could say, something that should be avoided at all times.

2017

Vincent van Gogh

The discovery

Entire villages make money from collections of a single artist. Nuenen, in the case of Vincent van Gogh, is a good example of this. There are municipalities that generate a large part of their income from tourism in which a certain artist plays a crucial role, think of Amsterdam with the Van Gogh Museum; it attracts people from all over the world.

Nuenen can also comment on this, they were considering expanding the museum to accommodate the enormous crowds of people. Especially at weekends, busloads of people from all over the world, as far away as China, wanting to see where Vincent van Gogh once lived. Often they don't even go inside, in many cases a photo with the museum in the background is enough, and strangely enough some people think an entrance ticket of six euros is too much money.

A lot has been written and released in terms of films about the life of Vincent van Gogh, and we are far from done talking.

In his time photography was barely developed. The upper class sometimes had a single portrait photo taken, then that was pretty much it.

Painting was a way to properly depict events, beautiful nature or people and in this way became somewhat outdated when photography was introduced on a large scale.

However, impressionism was a great way for the painter to give his own twist to what he saw, the atmosphere he could create was not only determined by the light, but also by the artist's emotions, which in the expressionism of a slightly later period even came to dominate.

As photography continued to develop, abstract art became increasingly prevalent.

Displaying a landscape had lost relevance for the artist; after all, there were photos that could be preserved for posterity. Although a painting can of course be much more decorative and beautiful on the wall than a simple photo, which in turn often does not match an original work on canvas in terms of value. Photos on the wall are without atmosphere, they are in fact a cheap decoration of a room, as they can be copied endlessly, unlike unique paintings on canvas.

Van Gogh must have thought the same way. The works he painted in France in particular, often provided a beautiful picture of the landscape at that time.

That was perhaps the greatest importance of his work, that now more than a century later we can still see how beautiful everything was then, in a special way, he could bring landscapes beautifully to life, it was the period just before the industrial revolution, which says enough.

I usually kept my eyes open at auctions and markets.

The first drawing I found was a charcoal portrait, probably made of Anna van Gogh-Carbentus, Vincent van Gogh's mother. I bought this from someone living in West Brabant. The work may have come from the Breda Chests, this name came about after Mrs. Van Gogh-Carbentus left Nuenen, her husband was a pastor and died young. She had to leave the parsonage and decided to return to West Brabant, where a large part of her family originally came from. Vincent had left the Netherlands at that time, never to return. There were a few chests in the parental home in which he had stored works, most of which were drawings and watercolors. Sometime later, Mrs. Kröller-Müller came into possession of some of the contents of the chests and with her collection she was able to found a beautiful museum on the Veluwe.

The crates had been lost, Vincent's mother had no room for the large crates in her small apartment, where she had moved with one of her daughters, and had to temporarily store them, during the move, with someone from Breda who had helped her. Eventually she moved to Delft and forgot about the chests. No one from the family ever found them again. Its contents were sold at markets years later, Vincent was not yet known and because of the often missing signature, the works were sold for a few guilders each. It may well be that the drawing came from one of these chests, later called the Breda Chests.

Ten years later I found the work mentioned earlier, an impression, impressionistic painting of the parsonage. It stood on the floor at the entrance of a thrift store, and it was immediately noticeable that it was well painted. I lifted it up and looked at it closely; it was framed in a white frame. A week later I went back, luckily it was still there, I also bought a Bible, coincidentally both were green in color, and predominantly green I must say about the painting.

Later I discovered that green was one of Vincent van Gogh's two favorite colors, the other being red, the combination of these two colors has a meaning, namely mercy. A quality that Vincent showed with dedication when he went into the shaft with miners in the Borinage and even donated part of his clothing to them. They had never had a stranger evangelist there before. He often received these kinds of reactions, for example when he attended an art academy in Belgium and developed a strange, angular style of his own because he found simply copying very boring. Vincent regularly incurred the wrath of the established order, and his father in particular showed aversion to his lifestyle. The rest of the family did not always agree with it either, and it made Vincent decide to leave The Netherlands shortly after his father died. He ended up in France via Belgium.

At that time I was not very concerned with the authenticity of the painting, it did not even occur to me at first that it could have been painted by Van Gogh. Although Nuenen is just around the corner from my hometown, it has been a blind spot for a long time. Of course I knew his work, and when I went to college the bus always stopped right in front of the house where the family lived at the time. The house that was certainly a great source of inspiration for this work. It was sometimes difficult to believe that he once lived so close by.

I thought his work was beautiful and painting had gradually become largely my life. The two above-mentioned finds made me decide to delve deeper into his work, and not without results, I also continued my search for paintings.

Art

I have been interested in art since I was sixteen and often visited museums as a child. Later I trained for creative therapy before I graduated from university, married the American abstract expressionist Richard Lee Barton and together with him I built up a collection of colorful, especially very large, beautiful works, where I chose the material and often also the ideas. My husband did the executive work, literally and figuratively very tough, no one will ever imitate him again, no matter how easy it seems.

Fortunately, many of his beautiful works have been preserved.

I have been custodian of the collection for more than twenty-five years now. I already had enough experience in the field of art, I was raised with it in my family, and I had taken painting lessons for years, including twenty years from Richard.

This basis for doing solid research seemed sufficient to me; as a graduated scientific researcher, I should be able to do that myself.

When I recently found a Japanese woodcut at the same site that I was quite sure must have been in Vincent's possession, the evidence was obvious, even though it had been for a long time.

In addition, I have learned a lot about Pieter Kruijsen, a man with whom Vincent van Gogh, when he lived in Nuenen - possibly later - had regular contact and who used to live practically around the corner from me, in exactly the opposite direction from Nuenen.

It is common for a painting to be called a Van Gogh as soon as the Van Gogh Museum issues a certificate for this. An almost impossible task to achieve. In the past, they received an average of one work per day with a request for research, but this will be much less from September this year. As a private individual you can no longer make a request, this can only be done through an art dealer. The working method has changed drastically, although I will still describe the course of events here until September.

To start with, photos had to be supplied in a format that was difficult to obtain, on the basis of which an assessment followed. Then, about six weeks later, which in itself suggested fairly thorough research, you received a standard rejection letter, with only one, not very compelling, argument.

In a very rare case they would ever conduct further research; images we know from TV usually relate to works from their own collection. Currently it has been made even more difficult, as a citizen you can no longer submit an application yourself, research now has to be arranged through an art dealer.

This method of research was taken very seriously worldwide, but in reality it was in many cases nothing more than a wash. In most cases there was no assessment of the work in real life. Even if you found four paintings in the same place, as I did, people seemed unable to make a connection, or rather, there was little interest or interest in it, in fact they saw it as competition, while the Van Gogh Museum is an institution subsidized by the Dutch government.

You would prefer to see Vincent rise from his eternal sleep to give his approval, although there are also plenty of painters who, years later, barely recognize some of their own works, and not the least sometimes, especially with a large oeuvre.

I do not want to elaborate further on the museum's policy here, it is clear that they have many other interests that do not always have to do with authentication, after all, the main task is to keep the museum running. You could almost conclude that political reasons partly determine whether a painting is real or not, absurdity at its finest! However, all of this is still taken very seriously worldwide.

The same standard rejection letter four times with a single argument, the same each time, is not very credible. It can only be called good expertise with great difficulty, for which they are really highly regarded worldwide. It clearly looks more like guesswork!

They need to be much clearer about the fact that their budget is not sufficient for research, because the reason they give is not enough time, something I can imagine a lot about, they are offered hundreds of works every year.

Yet they continue to say that they are the designated authority at world level for the authentication of paintings by Vincent van Gogh that is the crux.

Many art dealers and auctioneers rely on this. You might think, almost wrongly, because they also say that they are only giving advice.

That only makes it worse.

Thorough research is suggested.

Many are familiar with the image of the famous painting with the bridge in France, or the Sunflowers that are carefully placed on a table in a studio by museum employees wearing white gloves.

In many cases, calibration does not extend beyond a white envelope with a rejection based on a few photos on the doormat.

It can almost be called misleading, they say they receive hundreds of applications every year and very rarely approve any of them. It seems as if only the interests of the museum count. It is understandable that you have to be careful in such matters, these are extremely valuable goods, but citizens also have rights, at least to be treated properly, I think.

The artist

Artists did not always want to put everything on paper. People had never heard of the certificates as we know them today, they preferred to put as little on paper as possible, and the profession was already difficult enough. People were often satisfied with a loaf of bread or something similar in exchange for a drawing.

A baker in Nuenen was a good example of this, he would regret it if he knew how much the drawings were worth that he threw one by one into his oven when Vincent came by again for a loaf of bread and no money had.

These types of stories are cherished in Nuenen, but every effort is made to prevent neighboring municipalities from benefiting from the financial gain that has come to them. Gemert, located about fifteen kilometers away, was the real artists' haven. A glory that did not belong to the Netherlands for a long time.

For six centuries, from twelve to eighteen hundred, it was a kind of no man's land and enclave of the then powerful Teutonic Order, also called The Free Lordship.

For about two centuries they were forced to join the Netherlands. They had their own laws, or rather none or very few laws; after all they were a free state.

When, coincidentally, in the same year that Vincent ended up in Nuenen, Gemert became accessible by a tram line from Helmond, the number of artists visiting Gemert only increased.

De Keizer tram station, where an establishment with the same name is still located, seemed to be the meeting point for people from far and wide who wanted to escape the then oppressive citizenship and make a profession of their greatest hobby: Painting.

The paintings

Charcoal portrait

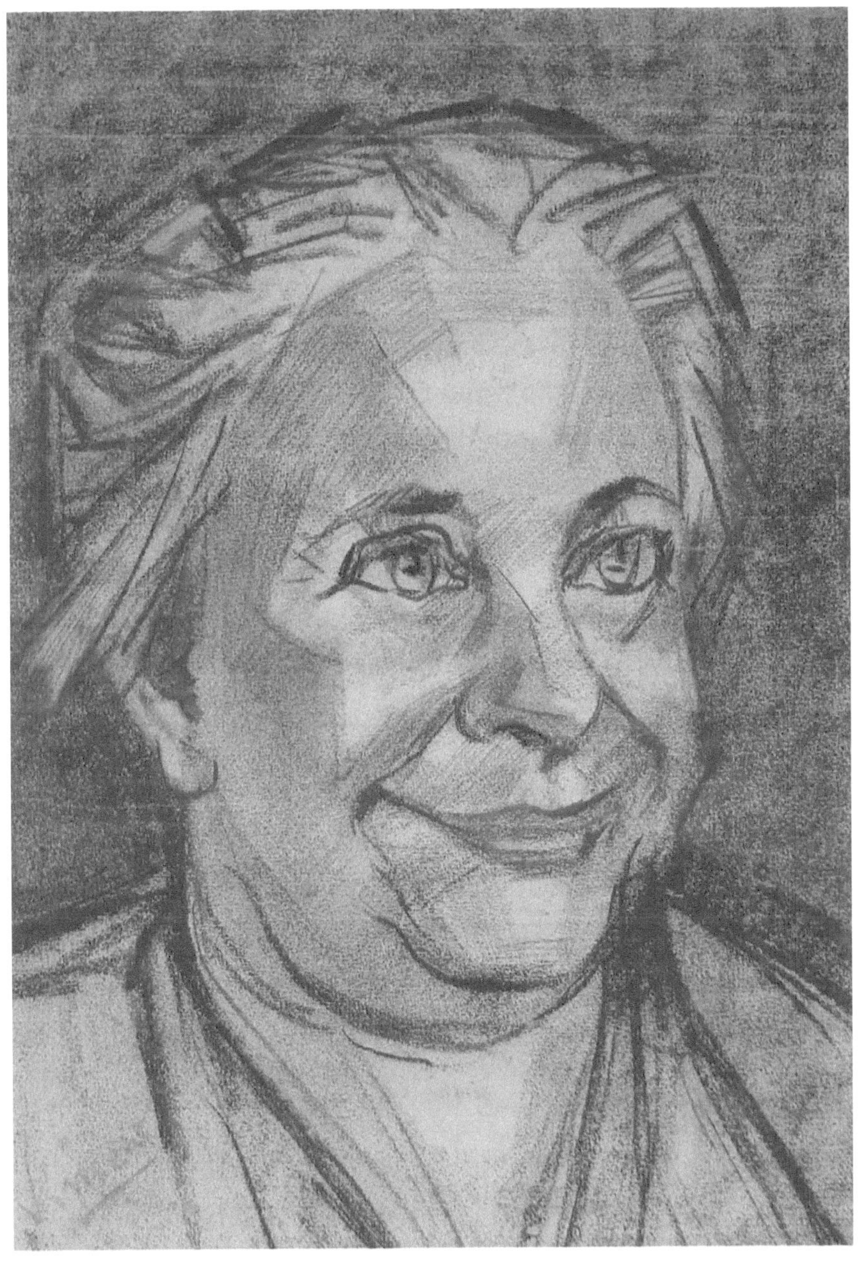

Anna van Gogh - Carbentus (1819 - 1907) laid the foundation for the development of Vincent's painting talent, not only through the drawing lessons she gave him, but also through the long walks she took with her children in nature, especially in the area of Zundert. It is almost inevitable that this is a drawing that Vincent made of his mother sometime in the early 1880s. His angular style was one of the reasons that he was no longer welcome at the Academy of Antwerp - where he went from Nuenen, only to never set foot on Dutch soil again. Very few images or photos of his mother are known.

Photography had just made its debut at that time and was therefore in direct competition with painting. Portrait and landscape painters in particular had to deal with this; something that was later of great importance for developments in art and directly contributed to the emergence of modern art could be related.

This meant there were fewer reasons to faithfully depict landscapes, objects, or whatever. Photography had taken its place and memories for posterity could now be captured on film.

Perhaps the reason why painters started to give their own interpretations to what they depicted on the canvas. This is how impressionism was born, also the first phase in the direction of modern art, an era of which Vincent was certainly a part. The subsequent major movement, namely expressionism, is clearly something that arose after his time, but for which he certainly planted the first seeds. Most characteristic in this respect are the works he made in Arles and St. Remy, which are also the most sought after.

The drawing in question was found near Breda and may have come from one of the chests that ended up in a storage facility somewhere after the death of Vincent's father and the later move of his mother from Nuenen to Breda, after which some time later its contents were offered for a small sum at various places, mainly flea markets and the like, so that Mrs. Kröller-Müller was able to build up part of her collection of Van Gogh's.

The work is drawn with charcoal on paper and signed at the bottom left. The paper does not appear to have a standard size; it was cut from a larger sheet, possibly from a sketchpad of a fairly large size, at least larger than A4, although this term did not yet exist at the time. A roll of paper seems illogical because the paper has no curve at all, it will have to be cut from a larger sheet, perhaps a loose sheet that could also be done. It is strong paper of good quality, although it was not acid-free paper given a single age spot, which is hardly visible to the naked eye.

All four sides have been cut, you could almost say. Although this is no longer visible because the work has been framed. In a very beautiful authentic, gold-colored frame (50 x 60 cm), with a beautiful dark red passe-partout with a beige inner cut in exactly the same color as the paper, which makes it a special whole with a monumental appearance, it is as if Mrs. van Gogh silently, without judgement, friendly.

The list was added later and from a slightly later period. The size of the drawing is approximately 26 x 36 cm, the style is exactly Van Gogh, the dark hatched background, and charcoal stripes as only Van Gogh managed to put them accurately on paper, exactly his way of working. The depth and what strikes me is the shape of the ear, but also the way the hair is drawn. A very beautiful drawing of a middle-aged woman, looking away but clearly posing. The work could very well have been made in Nuenen.

She is clearly not a woman of peasant descent, the lines in her face show intelligence. Something that Vincent's mother certainly had in her, she regularly accompanied her husband, who was a pastor, on home visits and was a welcome guest everywhere.

From the looks of it she was happy, which could mean that the drawing was drawn at the end of the nineteenth century, when everyone was still a bit happy that Vincent returned to the parental home. Shortly afterwards she broke her hip, which does not alter the fact that someone would nevertheless be able to laugh very cheerfully again after a period of recovery, but that aside, in the photo she radiates pure joy, not the face of a woman who suffered a major tragedy recently.

The date could therefore be a little later, summer 1884, although it does not have a summer atmosphere at all and later in the year the problems surrounding Vincent's stay piled up, there was not much to laugh about anymore, you could say. The portrait shows a spontaneous appearance, reason to date it at the end of 1883, beginning of 1884. It is most logical to assume that Mrs. Van Gogh started posing for Vincent before she fell down at Eeneind station in Nuenen and broke her hip, then a worrying period began, in this case there is no sign of pain on her face, December 1883 is the most logical date. The Christmas season was a special period for the Van Gogh family, everyone was happy to see each other again, and the holidays were celebrated exuberantly in the family circle. If you look at the drawing longer, you would almost say that she has crawled away from the Christmas tree. Smiling so happily, it may also have been the only time of year when there was room for such activities as posing for a portrait drawing.

The period preceding painting with water and later oil paint was a time when Vincent conceived the idea of becoming an artist himself, after working for years in his uncle's art business. His brother Theo also worked as an art dealer for Goupil & Cie, whose branch in The Hague was once set up by their uncle Vincent, also known as Uncle Cent; you can guess where this nickname comes from.

Uncle Cent had no children of his own and took care of his godson Vincent with love. When you talk about money, the profession of art dealer naturally had more prestige than that of a pastor. The family had a lot of standing, many of them had once ended up in evangelization, others in the art world as art dealers.

In his mid-twenties, Vincent increasingly began to realize that the profession of art dealer he had ended up in suited him even less than the call to become an evangelist, something to which he was attracted but also ended in a fiasco, which you can partly say about his.

He could not earn his living with it, but the beauty of the works was all the greater.

Perhaps the most special thing is that many of his landscapes were created in the period when industrialization was still in its infancy, which gives one a good idea of nature a century and a half ago. In a word, beautiful, man has destroyed so much, people thought they would get better but only went backwards, something that cannot be reversed.

As far as I am concerned, that is the strength of many of Van Gogh's works, in addition to the fabulous use of color, to which his mother certainly contributed with her half sewing workshop, embroidery and sewing used to be for ladies, in this case in particular for Vincent's sisters, a common pastime. It seems that he was able to acquire a lot of color knowledge with spools of thread. There is often a particularly strong color contrast, something that gives his works enormous power and appearance, think of the famous bridge in the south of France, the Bridge of Langlois. Everyone probably remembers it, the bright yellow and blue exactly in the primary colors, you couldn't have a stronger contrast. To apply such use of color in a painting you need a lot of color knowledge. Because he drew a lot prior to painting, his paintings gained a lot of power, one of the reasons why his popularity is still immense.

Pastor's house

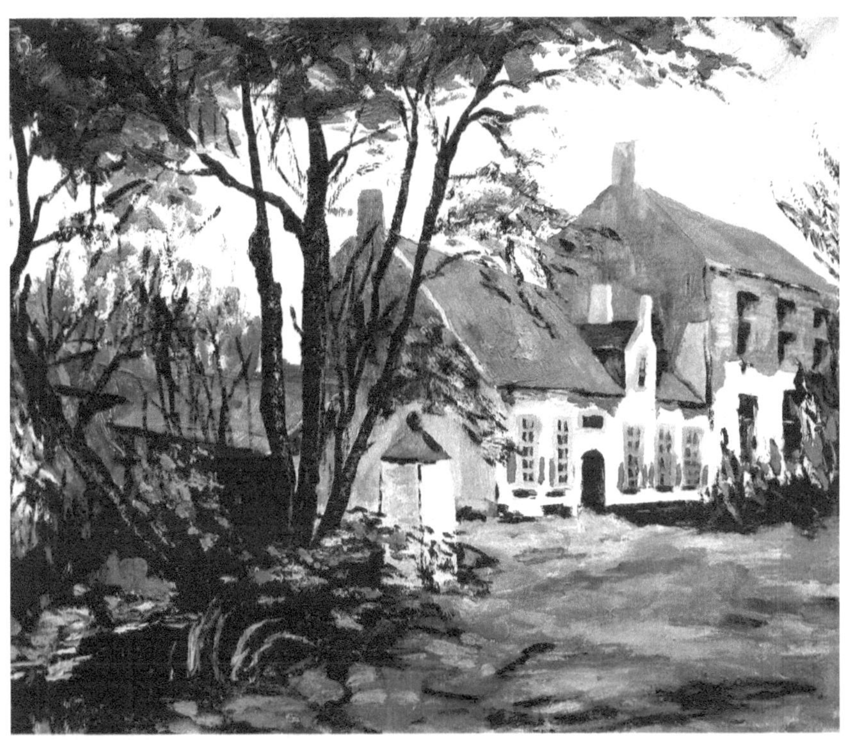

The house in the painting Pastor's House resembles one of the houses where Vincent van Gogh lived in the Borinage, namely the house of evangelist Edouard Francq in Cuesmes.

It also shows similarities with the house of the Denis family in Petit-Wasmes, where he previously lived in the southern Belgian mining region, that house had red walls and green shutters.

But it is perhaps most similar to the pastor's house in Nuenen, and was probably the house he remembered wistfully at that moment. If you look closely, many shapes of the actual house are reflected in the painting, and there are many similarities with other works that show a house with a similar design.

His fascination with the colors red and green, as can also be read in letter number one hundred and twenty-seven, becomes clear here, as does the presence of white and black, which he also spoke about in the aforementioned letter, which was written during his stay in the Borinage, where the white reminded me of the snow. The black could symbolize black gold or coal, the extraction of which is a dark page in history.

Before he left for Belgium and stayed in England, he already spoke about red and green, the colors of mercy, as mentioned earlier in one of the previous chapters.

The extension in the painting is reminiscent of the wash house of the real pastor's house, where he temporarily had a studio, it also had a round arch at the entrance, the shed in the backyard also shows a striking similarity, and it hangs a bit crooked on.

A later work by Vincent, namely Rue d'Auvers-sur-Oise (1890), is very similar to this work and can easily be called a more flamboyant version, clearly painted in a slightly later period, but with a similar perspective, the same color schemes and a similar brushstroke, although time of course also brought changes. Both show similarities with the pastor's house, if you pay attention.

Van Gogh drew Maison Magros sometime in the late 1870s. It also looks a lot like the house in this painting. Many similarities can also be seen in House Zandmennik from the same period, here too there are terraced buildings and dormer windows.

In terms of color and perspective, one also sees similarities in the White House at Night (1890); a similar color of green appears frequently and the pillars in front of the house have exactly the same shape, the viewpoint or the place from which the house is painted is also similar.

At La Maison Jaune (1888) you see the same perspective, as well as the layout; a smaller house in the foreground, a larger one behind it and something attached to it to the side, it also has an enormous depth which makes the work so special, you can also see the light color green here again, as well as round arches and shutters.

The Van Gogh family was hit by one serious tragedy after another. Perhaps it started with his mother's leg fracture, shortly after Vincent arrived in Nuenen.

She had a complicated serious bone fracture exactly below the hip joint; she was able to do very little for months.

People sometimes wonder why he stopped his education halfway through high school; it was exactly when he turned sixteen, which could have been for financial reasons, because at that time he was no longer required to attend school. His father's income was not very generous as a pastor (an honorable position that is) and they had a large family, it was later Theo who, at least for Vincent, kept things running. Vincent did not want to know much about the academy in Den Bosch, which already existed at the time, because according to him it had little to do with real painting. But this is beside the point.

Find an image of the drawing: Flowering Chestnut Trees at a House (1890). It looks a lot like a sketch for the Minister's House, the tree in the foreground, the house behind it, the pillar.

All this leads to the suspicion that the Pastor's House must have been painted later. Possibly in Auvers-Sur-Oise when Vincent had already left the south of France, the resemblance to Flowering Chestnut Trees is striking.

Still life with blue clogs

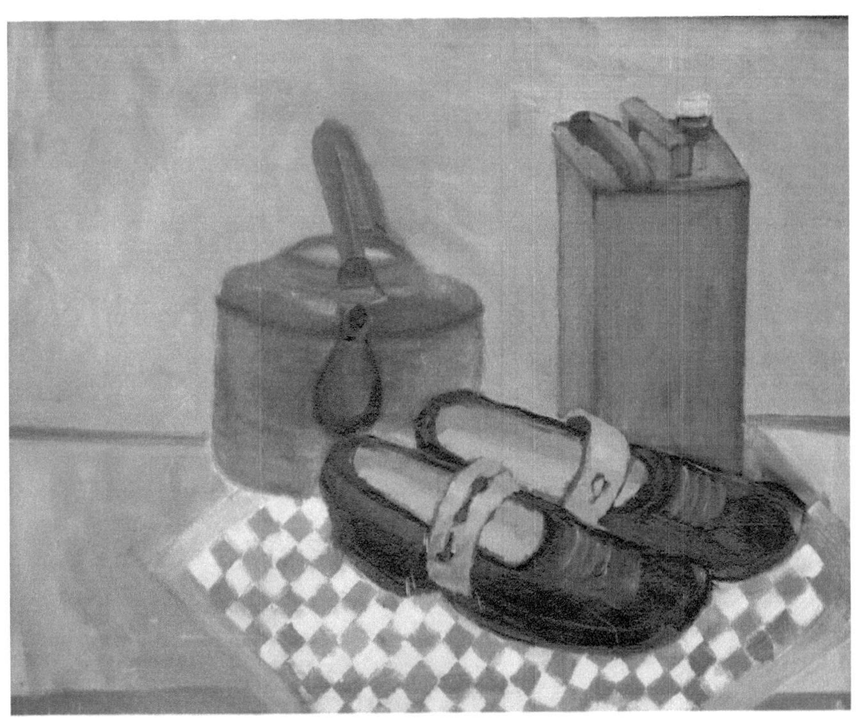

You regularly see in the work of Vincent van Gogh that the center line that gives the work perspective and also divides surfaces, is not completely straight in the sense that it not only sometimes slopes downwards from left to right to a greater or lesser extent, but also does not run completely straight when an object such as a vase or the like falls in front of it.

This is visible in some paintings with sunflowers, he painted several. Perhaps the Still Life with Blue Clogs and Scull should also be dated to the same period, as they have the same characteristics.

The still life also has a horizontal line that is quite thin but has a certain width of about one centimeter.

You also see this more often in that period, not only in the Sunflowers but also in a well-known self-portrait painted in 1887, which also has the same yellow colors next to the fairly broad line that gives the work perspective. The Sunflowers were painted in Arles in the late 1880s, as were some of his sculls.

Perhaps this work reflects how meager Vincent's possessions were at one time. Like Scull, this work may also have been painted over another; here you see contours of figures or perhaps a landscape in the background.

At that time there were few images, photography was hardly available.

To be able to paint a work like Scull you really need a good example. There were those in Huize Padua, but Dr. Gachet may have had one too. The first thing you notice when you enter the museum in Boekel is a 'lifelike' skull in a beautifully designed display case.

Vincent was often dressed in blue, which may be why he used the different color blue for the clogs in the still life. I recently saw Vincent's original painting shoes in Museum Vincentre: Blue in color!

The three works on canvas depict both desire and fear. Homesick for Brabant and the period in Nuenen, but also melancholy and illness. Perhaps all three were painted in Arles. During that period he also painted houses reminiscent of his parental home, some of which were in a fairly technical style.

Skull

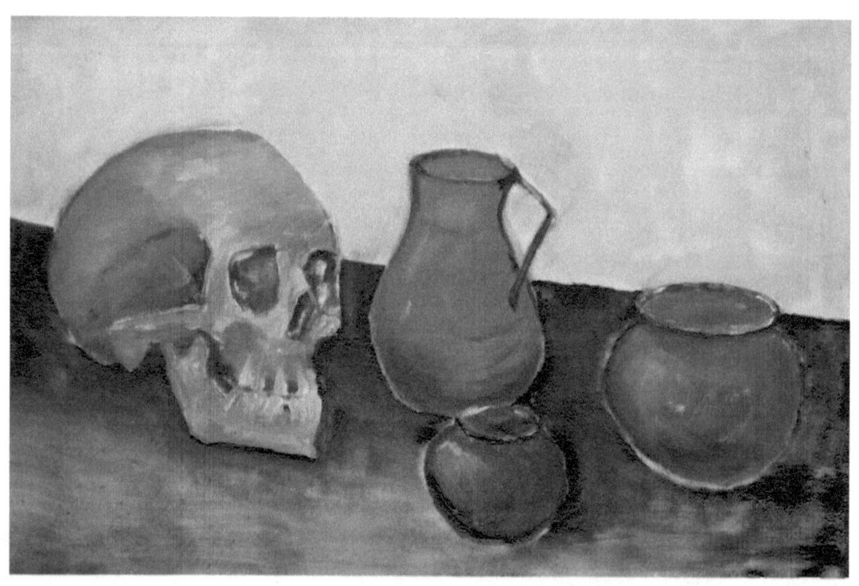

In psychiatry at that time, a common treatment method was to surgically remove mucus from the brain. It was thought that removing cerebrospinal fluid could remove the condition of insanity. Fortunately, there are better methods today.

Reverend Dorus van Gogh threatened Vincent with forced admission, which must have been very frightening for him, it may be the reason he started painting skulls, which is no small feat, and something you definitely need an example for.

Given the fact that real skulls could be found in both Huize Padua and Dr. Gachet's, it is logical to assume that the painting was painted in one of the two places.

This work could be the first of a series, or the last.

When he left Nuenen for Paris, he also painted skulls there, so it is not the case that he only started with Dr. Gachet.

Apparently he had already gained the necessary inspiration somewhere before.

There was hardly any photography at that time and this skull was most likely painted based on a real example. Perhaps he later realized that a skull alone fills the canvas enough.

The skulls give a terrifying appearance.

In the many still life's with flowers, Vincent painted pots and vases in all kinds of strange shapes. A kind of sloping diameter that gives the impression of a table or something similar is also no exception.

The main feature of this is that the line slopes downwards.

You can see it clearly in the Sunflower paintings, but even better in the work in question.

Perhaps Vincent wanted to indicate the relativity of life in this way, which was not always welcomed. An understatement!

The shape of the pots in his Sunflower paintings is the same as that of the small round pots in Scull. The yellow color is equally striking, a color he used a lot in the late 1980s, at the end of his painting life. It is therefore no coincidence that the painting discussed in the next chapter has the same yellow color.

Vincent was an avid traveler and liked to take the train, even if he hardly had any money he would still go on a trip for a week.

In Handel near Huize Padua there is a house where Maria Kruijsen lived, she was the brother of Antoon and daughter of Jan Kruijsen. All members of the famous Brabant expressionist family. In Oirschot you have the Kruysenhuis. Many Kruijsens lived not only in the Boekel-Uden area, but also a little further towards Tilburg-Boxtel.

Jan Kruijsen's father was a railway employee, which made it easier for family members to take the train at that time. Huize Padua was a center for painters, art played an important role in treatments and artists were regularly admitted there. Not only was it a very difficult subject, the presence of good materials, professional teachers and good accommodation facilities also had a certain appeal.

A few hundred meters from the house in Handel where Maria Kruijsen lived is the house where Henri Bol lived, he was also from a well-known painting family and worked as a painting therapist at Huize Padua.

Paul Gaugain also painted some skulls, from the style you can immediately see that the work was by another painter.

Old bridge Gemert

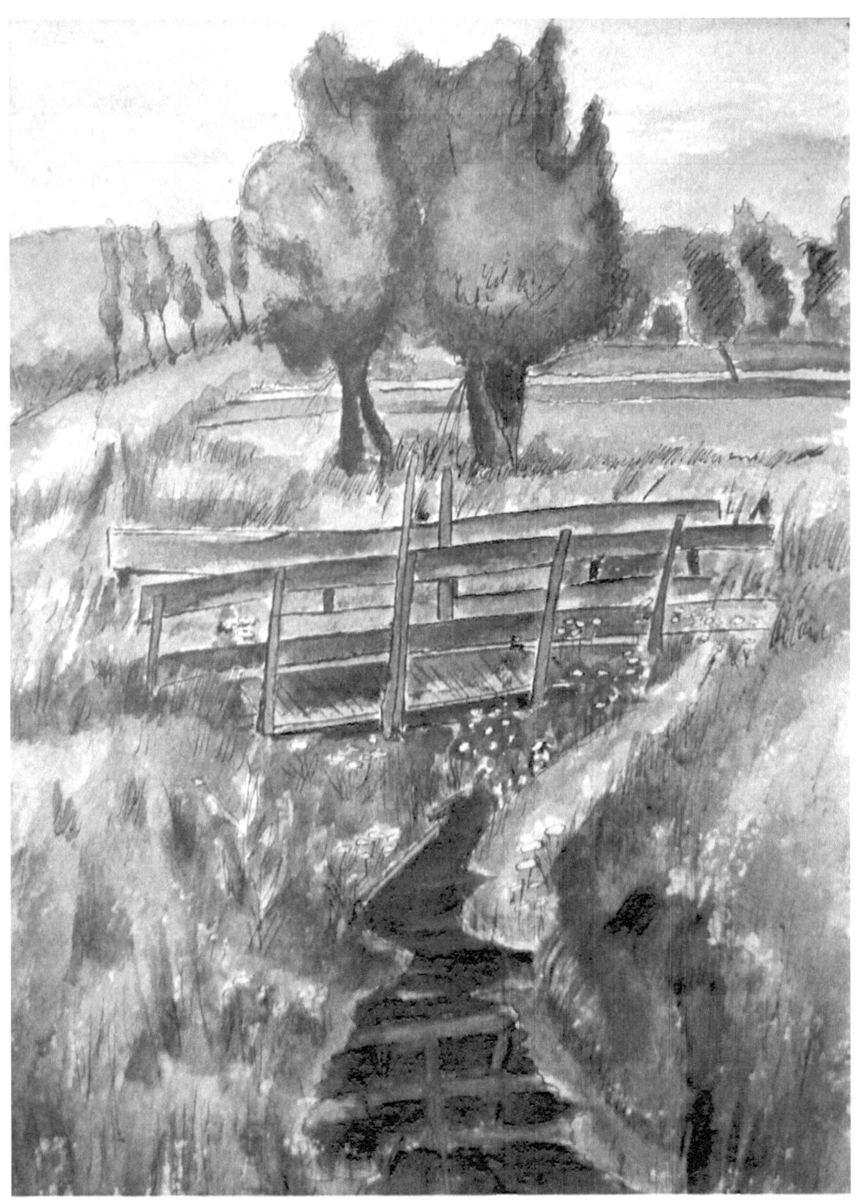

Once again found a work in the same environment, the style of which is suspiciously similar to that of Van Gogh. At that time he regularly wandered around Nuenen, it often happened that he only came home to eat and sleep, or not at all. Someone said that he was sometimes away from home for weeks.

On the old pass-partout of this work, which is still cut in a straight line, not an oblique cut, it is written 'old bridge Gemert'. Painted in a flamboyant, typical Van Gogh style. The work is painted on thick watercolor paper using watercolor paint and ink; it has some small age spots that are barely visible.

The horizon is high in the sky, the landscape is much layered and many shades of green have been used. In the top left corner a row of poplars. You are, as it were, sucked in, it has such depth.

What is striking is the use of small circles to give the work a playful impression. You see this more often in Van Gogh's works in that period, you could say the beginning of pointillism, which later turned into all kinds of striped patterns, which are also recognizably present here.

The ink patterns are exactly the same as those in the ink drawings of the Nuenen period, which is very telling.

You see this more often in Vincent's work in that period, especially in the ink drawings he made in Nuenen you see many vertical to diagonal stripes, as you also see in this work. However, in this watercolor the circles have also been added.

The sketch of the world-famous painting Portrait of Dr. Gachet shows shapes that are also visible in Oud bruggetje Gemert, namely half to full circles and dashes. When Vincent stayed in a sanatorium in the south of

France, he painted an enormous amount, and material must certainly have been available there.

A period that ends where it began, namely with different stripe patterns, although heavily painted in this later period.

In one of his letters, Vincent mentions that he sometimes walks for hours through the fields with someone from Nuenen. This way he could easily have ended up in Gemert and the surrounding area.

This work was found in the same place, but not in the same period. It is actually from a different period than, for example, Domineeshuis.

During that time he made two drawings that can serve as supporting evidence:

- The Kingfisher;
- Behind the Hedges.

Both are also made in ink and paint on wove paper.

They show long hedges, also typical of the natural character of Gemert at that time.

These hedges were planted exactly on De Peelrand, a geographical fault line that runs from approximately Asten to Gemert towards Uden and Heesch.

In Gemert, construction started to the west of the fault line, in the east there was a large nature reserve, namely De Peel, which was located behind the hedge.

De Haag is still a street name in Gemert and, how coincidentally, the oldest street in Gemert.

From the hedge people went into nature to hunt and the swampy area was also used for cutting peat.

West of the hedge the grass was really greener, and a street in question is still called De Heuvel, possibly this is where the well-known expression comes from, in this case related to the geographical location and also one of the oldest streets in Gemert .

Gemert was a so-called ribbon village, and consisted of a long main road with a hedge on one side exactly on the fault line.

In the IJsvogel you see the first signs of buildings on the east side of the hedge; on the west side you see the church of Gemert, with a little imagination.

Achter de Heggen could be located on the southwest side of Gemert, near the gatehouse of the castle. The same lines in the landscape and light are still visible today, especially because the village on that side of Gemert has not changed much over the centuries.

In the watercolor in question here you see the first forms of cypresses, a row of trees built very closely together on the Boekelseweg, they are still there, and furthermore you see the typical layering of the landscape and a high horizon.

A painter can get inspiration from anywhere. It may happen that at night you dream that the Eiffel Tower is in your backyard. When you wake up and look out the window, it turns out to still be the mill that was installed there decades ago. However, it might inspire you to paint a tower behind your house. Artists often have a lot of imagination, which is sometimes difficult for the average citizen to understand.

Poplar Avenue near Nuenen

Vincent van Gogh painted two versions of this painting, as he often did, with the help of his painter friend Anton Kerssemakers. One of the two works is owned by Museum Boijmans van Beuningen, I describe the other here.

During the period that he stayed in Nuenen, Vincent at some point met Antoon Kerssemakers, also known as Toon Kers, a painter from Eindhoven, Gestel actually. They had regular contact with each other and Vincent occasionally gave him some painting lessons. Then Toon Kers came to visit Vincent in the studio of sexton Schafrath in Gerwen and they went out together.

It often happened that on these occasions they painted the same object as an example for a still life, or they painted two identical works in nature from exactly the same point of view.

A good example of this is the work Autumn Landscape, one of which is in the collection of the Kröller-Müller Museum, the other in a private collection. Two versions are also known of Symphony in Yellow, which later became known as Populierenlaan near Nuenen and is in the possession of Museum Boijmans van Beuningen.

When Vincent van Gogh left the Netherlands after the death of his father, never to return, he gave Toon Kerssemakers a painting as a gift, namely Autumn Landscape.

This is described in the well-known articles that were co-authored by Toon Kerssemakers in the weekly magazine De Amsterdammer, written at the beginning of the last century.

The painting Autumn Landscape in the possession of Museum Kröller-Müller does not have the dimensions as described in the above article, it is smaller. The second version painted by Toon Kers is even smaller. Symphony in Geel does have that size.

"Vincent worked over autumn landscape in Paris in 1886," says Andries Bonger, a good friend and later brother-in-law of Theo van Gogh, Vincent's brother - this is described in a booklet written by art historian Mrs. Tellegen-Hoogendoorn.

He must have meant another painting here, namely Symphony in Yellow, which was later called Populierenlaan near Nuenen. Symphony in Yellow was sold to Museum Boijmans van Beuningen; he took the other version of this work to Paris and worked on it further by applying an extra layer of paint to the horizon. This work is different, softer in color and more detailed, it has a different size than the work in the museum and less of a yellow glow. Symphony in Geel would therefore have been a very good title for the painting that Museum Boijmans van Beuningen has in its collection.

With special thanks to Mr. T. de Brouwer, in his book Van Gogh and Nuenen, he also discusses this subject, albeit based on a different painting, but from the same point of view. The confusing thing about the whole story is that several books describe that Vincent took Autumn Landscape with him to Paris and worked another layer over it; this is recognized by historians and even by Vincent's immediate family.

A mistake probably occurred here; he took Populierenlaan near Nuenen with him to Paris and continued to work on it, the line on the horizon, which was added later, in the work in question here, and in my possession, clearly visible on the backside. It can be said with certainty that there were two works with the title Autumn Landscape and now a second one has been discovered with the title Populierenlaan near Nuenen, this had probably been forgotten and, perhaps due to the problems described above, somewhere in an attic ended up.

If you look over the painting you can see the old layer of paint that has been worked over it, which Andries Bonger was talking about, it is also clearly visible on the backside of the painting.

The Van Gogh works in my collection are in a safe in a secret location, they can be viewed by appointment if interested.

The research

Pieter Kruijsen

One day someone came to me and told me that the paintings that I suspected might have been painted by Vincent van Gogh might indeed be by him. This man had worked for a quarter of a century as a manager at Huize Padua, a home where Pieter Kruijsen, on whom my research later focused, also worked.

Pieter Kruijsen was once a pharmacist there, probably working in the in-house pharmacy, and also founded the painting department there. He lived in Erp for a while. The man who told me all this on a Sunday afternoon in Museum De Kluis had brought someone with him at the time of that conversation. This lady in question confirmed the same stories independently of him. These had come to her through tradition, grandparents or great-aunts and the like who had told her about them. She added to the story that Vincent had a nickname in Gemert, which the hamlet of Huize Padua borders. You don't just have a nickname, you really have to have been somewhere before. The man said that Vincent van Gogh regularly stayed with Pieter Kruijsen and his wife in Erp when he had problems at home in Nuenen. Nuenen is not far from Gemert and Erp, these places were easy to reach for Vincent van Gogh because there was already public transport at that time, and he could also have covered the distance on foot.

I recently bought a work by someone called Woltering. It often happens that people offer works for sales that have been rejected by the Van Gogh Museum, but were nevertheless painted by Vincent van Gogh.

Through genealogical research I discovered that the name Woltering regularly appears in publications about the Kruijsen family. There must also have been ties between these families. They had a clothing store in Lieshout, which is close to Nuenen.

My interest in this subject had been aroused much earlier when, in the apartment complex with the literal name Vrije Heerlijckheid, a lady came to me with the story that she knew someone within her family with ten Van Gogh paintings in the attic. This lady worked in the clothing business for a long time and later moved, but the next day she showed me one of those works, it was small and very old. Mrs. van Gogh apparently once exchanged them for garden furniture.

It could just as well be that art was exchanged for clothing, the name Woltering also occurred in Gemert, also related to clothing.

In Boekel, where I found works during the renovation of the town hall, successive mayors with the names Schafrath and Kruijsen were employed at that time, and they may have left paintings in the attic.

The name Schafrath is also a well-known name in the story about Vincent van Gogh because the sexton where he was temporarily housed in Nuenen also bore this name.

The Van Gogh Museum is highly regarded worldwide for research. Something that does not correspond to reality when you talk about research into authenticity in the broadest sense of the word, the research may not be objective enough and other factors play a role. This is a government-subsidized institution.

I once requested research for four paintings. These have been briefly examined separately using photographs. Four times I received the same standard rejection with one meaningless argument. When I called the museum's senior researcher about it, he hung up the phone within a minute. In my search for evidence I have come across many irregularities.

The fact is also that the Van Gogh family, which had partly rejected Vincent at that time, did not want to know anything about many of his contacts. Huize Padua was a taboo, if only because of the term psychiatry, which people did not want to use publicly.

As a result, there was a lot of censorship of the letters. And it is precisely the letters on which almost all books about Vincent van Gogh are based.

Moreover, during his stay in Nuenen he was close to his family, which made writing letters less necessary. The events of that period were also so intense that writing letters may not have been the first thing that came to mind.

It is known that Reverend van Gogh wanted to have his son admitted to Huize Padua before they moved to Nuenen. The choice of Nuenen may have played a role in this because of its favorable location in relation to Gemert.

In the year in which Vincent van Gogh joined his family in Nuenen, a tram line was even built from Helmond to Den Bosch. Helmond station could already be reached by train from Nuenen. The tram stopped in Gemert at De Keizer tram station, a place where painters gathered and where a certain Kruijsen later also held sway. There was also a tram station in Erp. The tram stopped not far from the house of Pieter Kruijsen. The story goes that Vincent was sometimes away from home for weeks because of problems and stayed with Pieter and his wife.

In any case, it is also certain that Lientje Kruijsen, or Geraldine, Pieter Kruijsen's daughter, had contact with Willemien, Vincent's youngest sister.

A number of the works were found in that area, during a period when the house where this Pieter Kruijsen once lived was cleared out and changed owners, which of course was no longer Pieter, you will understand. It was the same period that the Boekel town hall was renovated. Items from both locations may have been taken to the thrift store, where I came across a number of works.

It was during the Nuenen period that Vincent started painting with oil paint, and his contact with Pieter certainly contributed to this.

Thorough research has shown that these works are among the last painted, at least part of them; Vincent must have painted them sometime during the last two years of his life.

The research has been going on for years, it involves approximately ten works! The Van Gogh Museum refused to take it seriously and it is currently no longer possible to apply as a private individual.

Line's father, also called Lientje, was called Pieter Kruijsen. He was born in 1825 in Bergen op Zoom and worked in the medical world. He eventually got a position at Huize Padua where he founded the painting department, lived in Erp at the time and also died there in 1905. This is literal proof that there were ties between the families mentioned.

The house where he lived was for sale, clearing it out could explain the discovery of a number of works, the thrift store was almost around the corner, you could say.

According to sources in Gemert, people who worked at Huize Padua, there were contacts between Pieter Kruijsen and Vincent van Gogh. He regularly visited Pieter Kruijsen and his wife. A further description of this can be found in the previous chapter.

The basis of most books about Vincent van Gogh is formed by letters to his brother Theo published by Jo van Gogh-Bongers, Theo's widow at the time.

The investigation has started by tracing the origin. The first of the six works found is a painting of a minister's house.

Through tradition, there are still people who can tell all kinds of stories about his life. The starting points of most books are the letters, which form a fixed history. From a historical perspective, stories that circulate are often more difficult to determine whether they are correct, although they may just as well be true or perhaps even contain more truth in certain cases. Vincent could manipulate, or write begging letters to his brother to get money, and sometimes he could tell it nicely. Of course he developed an extraordinary talent for painting in his life, but I am not talking about that in this case.

The research focused on the Nuenen area, because he painted important works there. It soon became clear that some of the stories told there were quite at odds with those in the neighboring village of Gemert, even though he must have been there regularly. The village where his parents lived for several years and neighboring places where he wandered around because of problems at home, but also to gain inspiration and enjoy the beautiful nature. It was therefore interesting to find out what the transport options were like in the area at the time. Someone at the Vincentre said: "He often covered distances on foot, but did not get further than Stiphout!" There really isn't much of that to it. Stiphout is located a few kilometers from Nuenen towards Helmond.

It was known that he liked to take the train, but he also sometimes took long walks and sometimes walked for six hours at a time. He describes this in one of the letters he wrote during the period he stayed in Drenthe, just before he left for Nuenen. He was therefore able to get much further even by walking. This is mentioned in his later letters that actually relate to the period in question. In one of the letters from the Nuenen period he writes to Theo that he is working on a donkey and a horse. The first for painting, and the second for riding probably. However, there is much more evidence that he was roaming the area at that time.

Not every painting found in an attic is a Van Gogh, let that be clear. However, as time went on, the evidence piled up.

The second work is a still life with blue clogs and a bottle of absinthe, the third a skull. The three paintings on canvas in question were not painted in Nuenen. Considering the color and use of color, they are from a later period. Vincent may have got them from France sent to his friend in Erp.

These works may have been painted in the south of France and ended up here through acquaintances that could also be possible. They can be dated several years before he died.

In any case, this book provides evidence that Vincent van Gogh regularly visited the Gemert-Erp area, so it is not surprising that works could have been found here.

Any association with Gemert and Boekel could have been avoided because there were already enough stories about psychiatry circulating and perhaps also because of medical confidentiality. Gemert has always been a Free Lord, was not part of the Netherlands for a long time, and valued hospitality and hospitality.

Later, several painters ended up in Huize Padua. Painting was not an easy profession and, especially at that time, it was almost impossible to earn a living from it. Professional painting materials were widely available, including decent easels and the like.

At that time, industrialists from the west came to Southeast Brabant because of the textile industry. The Van Gogh family will have followed in their wake; Vincent's father was appointed as pastor to succeed his predecessor Begemann.

Brabant became predominantly Catholic at some point, but there was a period when there were fairly large Protestant communities, especially in the Uden, Veghel and Den Bosch area.

The tram line was built when Vincent joined the family, in exactly the same year; his parents had already lived in Nuenen a little longer.

Den Bosch wanted a railway line from Helmond. Eindhoven won the battle, as an alternative a tram started running on the said route.

It is sometimes difficult to say where a painter gets inspiration from. He gets images in his head that he wants to portray on the canvas.

One thing is certain, at some point Vincent started using a broader color palette, which is logical because he gained more and more experience with painting in oil. It may also have had to do with his mood, the presence of other materials, painting lessons, inspiration or mind-expanding substances. We can't ask him anymore!

This becomes especially visible when he leaves Nuenen and goes to live somewhere else.

There was a poplar avenue on the grounds of Huize Padua, there is a walking path on the bank of a small river with poplars on both sides, that path really appeals to the imagination.

If you were to go from there towards Nuenen, whether by horse, bicycle or on foot, you would pass a chapel that looks a lot like the Van Gogh church, namely the Spijkerkapel, where you can offer nails to Christ to thank God and ask for healing.

A painter gets ideas everywhere; everything can be a source of inspiration.

The letters can give a very colored picture of reality. Money was an important reason for Vincent to write the letters, after all his brother Theo provided him with his maintenance. Moreover, there was a complete history of illness, which means that certain periods and events may have been concealed. Privacy may have played a role in this, as could medical confidentiality.

The research in question here focuses on the Gemert-Boekel-Erp area. For Vincent, this region, located near Nuenen, was apparently a refuge at that time. Many more artists lived and visited there. In particular, Huize Padua, a psychiatric institution with a centuries-old history, was a cultural center for art.

A number of people have told me about this and it must be the reason that the works were found in this area. The fact that it was not openly discussed may have had a lot to do with the taboo on mental illness. Reverend Dorus van Gogh wanted to have his son Vincent admitted to Huize Padua. In any case, it is certain that Vincent had contact with Kruijsen, who worked there and had a prominent position. From Nuenen Vincent could take the train to Helmond from where he could travel by tram to Gemert and Erp. Kruijsen lived between Erp and Veghel. The tram drove past his house. Vincent regularly came home to Kruijsen and his wife and sometimes stayed there for a longer period of time, especially when he had problems with his parents, Vincent was sometimes away from home for weeks. Gemert was an agricultural weaving village. Nuenen had some industry in the form of breweries and later the clog making industry developed.

Schafrath

After a lot of wanderings, Vincent ended up with his parents in Etten in the early 1980s, after which he quickly left to settle in The Hague, where things also went wrong after some time, the next stop was Drenthe. Vincent did not last long there either and moved back in with his parents who had also moved, perhaps for a certain reason Reverend Van Gogh, Vincent's father, had accepted a position in Nuenen. Following the problems Vincent caused in The Hague, he had been thinking about having him admitted to a psychiatric institution for some time. In Boekel, not far from Nuenen, there was Huize Padua, a home where many painters once sought refuge. Precisely during the period when Vincent was staying with his parents, a professional painting department was founded, whether this was a coincidence we may never know, as there is still a heavy taboo on psychiatry, which was even worse at that time.

You could say that no further statements should be made about it, these are sensitive matters that affect medical confidentiality, although it was a long time ago, if it were not for the fact that Vincent van Gogh is a public figure, especially posthumously, although he performed during his life also likes to be in the foreground. The problem lies in the fact that it is precisely the ties with the institution that provide evidence, the Van Gogh family may not like it as much, but this also concerns financial interests, not just the private interests of the Van Gogh family, and everyone already knew how Life was difficult for Vincent at times, that is common knowledge

The fact is that various works were found in Boekel, at the time of the renovation of the town hall, where a Kruijsen once was mayor. The name

Schafrath also appeared, in the area there was a doctor with that name and yes, also a mayor, in exactly the same town hall.

The sexton in Nuenen, as you may know, from whom Vincent rented a studio, was also called Schafrath, hence this example.

It is a thing of the past to bend history to your will, in this day and age we want the complete truth and not in a way that suits someone better. You can make an honest judgment if you know everything, the image that is created may partly overlap with the truth, and there has been censorship.

The old bridge near Gemert was also found in Boekel and has exactly the style of Vincent van Gogh. In many ways, in terms of use of color, depth and type of paper. The paint and ink used correspond to a work from the same period, once owned by a Nuenen councilor and more or less recognized as Van Gogh by the museum. More about this later, because I was able to buy a drawing of a plowing farmer for a friendly price from the former alderman, stuck to a newspaper article from the nineteenth century.

I found the old bridge near Gemert in the same place and in the same period as three other works of which I strongly suspect that Vincent was the painter: a Scull; Still life with blue clogs; and the minister's house in red and green. The still life was clearly painted in the Arles period, it has the same yellow and red tones that he often used in that period, but it is especially the background that is strongly reminiscent of Van Gogh and also typifies the Sunflowers. Not only that, Scull has a number of pots as a still life that can be characterized exactly as the Van Gogh style in terms of shape and the downward line in the background is a shape that you actually never see in any other painter. It is known that Van Gogh made works during that period that reminded him of Nuenen, so the minister's house may have been created at a time when he was very ill and must have been fully aware of this, painted in his favorite colors red and green.

I have ten works in total, obtaining papers is a completely different story, the Van Gogh Museum is seen worldwide as the authority in the field of authentication, the Van Gogh family keeps an eye on things in the background, outsiders have little chance. You can be sure, you won't get any papers, and there are a lot of complaints about this, not just in the Netherlands. Professor Blanc from Switzerland agreed with me, he had been researching this for much longer, it seems as if other reasons, for example political ones, play an important role and that sometimes works are approved that were not even painted by Van Gogh.

Very little of what they were doing was actually correct, and recently they have made the admission to procedures much more complicated, it is initially an assessment based on photos, with no further explanation and provenance required. The fact is that they are leading, it is almost impossible to sell a Van Gogh without papers, presenting a certificate when selling is not an obligation but customary, at the same time there is a lot of criticism worldwide about the museum's working methods, the research, especially the first admission can almost be called worthless.

Van Gogh had mental problems and visited the Gemert-Boekel-Erp area regularly. This is not recognized because of contacts with the psychiatric institution, they did not want anything to come out about it. I've been researching this for years, people have told me a lot about it. The evidence pile

Obviously, there has been a lot of tampering in the past, which may be the reason why it is a closed stronghold.

The business of artists to sell works sometimes goes through narrow bends, that was no different with Van Gogh's works, people sometimes did the craziest things to sell a work, in the case of inheritances this can still be a lot Worse, family often has much less knowledge of selling art and thinks they can arrange it all.

I think it is very important to be 100 percent honest about this. One of the works I have is Populierenlaan near Nuenen, Boijmans van Beuningen has a copy of it, probably made by Toon Kers at that time, these are difficult issues, you can read more about them on my website, I report on years of research. I also found four works in the same place, near Erp where a good friend of Vincent lived, the Van Gogh family does not want to reveal anything about this either, I will show one of these four works in a vlog on my YouTube channel. I also have a charcoal drawing from the Breda chests; a painting made in Drenthe; a drawing from the former councilor of Nuenen; too many to mention actually. I once came across it by chance and thought it would be interesting to expand my art collection with works by Vincent, that's how it started years ago.

Vincent had a good friend who lived in Erp, he probably went there by tram, and then he took the train from Eeneind station to Helmond, where he could change to the line to Den Bosch. This stopped at De Keizer tram station in Gemert, a place where artists from the area gathered, and the tram also stopped in Erp. Today I will show you part of the route, which is still mainly nature reserves consisting of forests and agricultural land. The route ran along an ancient road that connected Oss and Asten, a road that lies on the peel fault edge, an area where geologically speaking tectonics meet. This used to be clearly visible in the landscape, but this is now less visible due to buildings. . East of the Peel Fracture Edge you had heathland and you ended up in the Peel, west of this edge was a much more fertile area and the grass on the other side of the hill was literally greener here, possibly this is where the expression comes from, there is a road called Heuvel and a side street of it is called Groenendaal. The heathland has been slowly reclaimed over the centuries, there is not much heath left, the hamlet of Verreheide still reminds of that time, it is located between Erp and Boekel, there are five enormous centuries-old Poplars in a row, a landmark in the landscape and also almost a symbol in some landscapes that Vincent painted, these poplars appear in the top left corner of several works. I will show you images of this in the next vlog, for now I am mainly concentrating on the tram route to Erp, nature, farms and also chapels along the way.

Pieter Kruijsen was once a pharmacist there, probably working in the in-house pharmacy, and founded the painting department there. He lived in Erp for a while. The man who told me all this on a Sunday afternoon in Museum De Kluis, had brought someone with him at the time of that conversation. This woman in question independently confirmed the same stories. These had come to her through tradition, grandparents or great-aunts and the like who had told her about them. She added to the story that Vincent had a nickname in Gemert, which the hamlet of Huize Padua borders. You don't just have a nickname, you really have to have been somewhere before.

The man told me that Vincent van Gogh regularly stayed with Pieter Kruijsen and his wife in Erp when he had problems at home in Nuenen. Nuenen is not far from Gemert and Erp, these places were easy to reach for Vincent van Gogh because there was already public transport at that time, and he could also have covered the distance on foot.

I recently bought a work by someone called Woltering. It often happens that people offer works for sales that have been rejected by the Van Gogh Museum but were nevertheless painted by Vincent van Gogh.

Through genealogical research I discovered that the name Woltering regularly appears in publications about the Kruijsen family. There must have been some ties between these families. I have found much more evidence for this.

In Boekel, where I found works at the time of the renovation of the town hall, successive mayors with the names Schafrath and Kruijsen were employed at that time. Through inheritance, paintings successively ended up possibly with one or more of the mayors. The name Schafrath is also a well-known name in the story about Vincent van Gogh because the sexton where he was given temporary shelter in Nuenen also bore this name.

The Van Gogh Museum is highly regarded worldwide for research. Something that does not correspond at all to reality when you talk about research into authenticity in the broadest sense of the word. It could even be that within this VVD stronghold, political colors determine authenticity even more than actual colors. Of course, something like this should not happen, as this is a government-subsidized institution.

I have requested research for four paintings. These have been briefly examined separately using photographs. Four times I received the same standard rejection with one meaningless argument. When I called senior researcher Van Tilborgh about it, he hung up the phone within minutes. In my search for evidence I have come across many irregularities.

The fact is also that the Van Gogh family, which had partly rejected Vincent at that time, did not want to know anything about many of his contacts. Huize Padua was a taboo, if only because of the term psychiatry, which people did not want to use publicly.

As a result, there was a lot of censorship of the letters. And it is precisely the letters on which almost all books about Vincent van Gogh are based.

Moreover, during his stay in Nuenen he was close to his family, which made writing letters less necessary. The events of that period were also so intense that writing letters may not have been the first thing that came to mind.

It is known that Reverend van Gogh wanted to have his son admitted to Huize Padua before they moved to Nuenen. The choice of Nuenen may have played a role in this because of its favorable location in relation to Gemert.

In the year in which Vincent van Gogh joined his family in Nuenen, a tram line was even built from Helmond to Den Bosch. Helmond station could already be reached by train from Nuenen. The tram stopped in Gemert at De Keizer tram station, a place where painters gathered and where a certain Kruijsen later also held sway. There was also a tram station in Erp.

In any case, it is also certain that Lientje Kruijsse, or Geraldine, Pieter Kruijsen's daughter, had contact with Willemien, Vincent's youngest sister.

The unmasking

I do not believe in a world without borders, there is a difference between good and evil, that is why we have a legal system; this is undermined, especially in Europe, by helping an endless stream of foreigners. People whose background is unknown, let alone their intentions, those who have God behind them are not alone. As a Christian you have billions of fellow Christians.

Perhaps the worst thing is that doctors, who often started studying medicine out of idealism, as the word says it all, end up disappointed. Ultimately they end up in a web of rules and are put under heavy pressure by managers, for example, as is the case in hospitals. Natural healing has even become prohibited, the legislator decides, the patient comes in third place and has no say anymore, it is a world that only revolves around money.

Doctors often only dare to give their opinion in anonymous back rooms, although in this case too, most are often selected for stupidity and compliance. The moment a doctor starts working somewhere, the recruitment process starts, they are showered with gifts, trips, and lease cars and so on. I know a clinic where the entire parking lot is full of Teslas, including charging points, the staff eats the patients' food, and the patient is served a bowl of oatmeal twice a day. All this could happen under the guise of the doctor being reliable, and it still is that way, the majority trust the doctor more than anyone else, while the patient is no longer in his interest. That is exactly what needs to change, pay the doctor as long as the patient is healthy, radically turn around the system, then things will turn around and healthcare costs can be more than halved.

Covid has been a preconceived plan with 5G as the cause of illness, the virus is the trigger. For example, Wuhan, where the trouble started, was the first city in the world to run entirely on 5G. They want to inject a chip into everyone, they need 5G for crowd control. At certain times the face masks were the most sickening, the vaccine will soon kill billions of people, it destroys your immune system, it is certainly not too late, anyway, but stop taking these injections.

There is something wrong with the system, I came across this during my research into the authenticity of the works of Vincent van Gogh, and something similar is happening in healthcare. Perhaps there is a common thread here.

2022

Carmen Barton

The French Alps

Together with Richard I regularly went to the Swiss or French Alps, initially we went camping, during later years we sometimes stayed in a friends' chalet.

In both France and Switzerland we knew someone who was willing to make a chalet available to us if it was empty. As is often the case in the summer months. A few hikers may still enjoy it high in the mountains, but the majority prefers to come in the winter.

We thought it would be nice to invite my sister and her family, they happened to be on holiday nearby, Italy to be precise. On the way back they would drive through France and come to us, we agreed.

That turned out to be quite a journey, on the map it sometimes seems like a piece of cake, but in reality, especially in mountainous areas, it can be quite disappointing.

After a day of waiting they arrived at the beginning of the evening. We had expected them around noon, we started eating the food that was ready for them because we were feeling faint, we wondered if they would come at all because we didn't hear anything from them.

They were slightly tipsy, it was noticeable, perhaps due to the thin mountain air, but probably mainly because of the alcoholic refreshments they had consumed during their luxurious, extensive lunch.

That had become their habit, expensive dining out, my sister said!

For that reason alone, it was completely unbelievable that her boyfriend, as he likes to be called, wanted to put spoiled leftovers in the refrigerator.

Meat products too, all brown and dirty, in an opened package. Leftovers of a few slices of which the expiration date was undoubtedly very far exceeded.

Or perhaps it was believable, unless you believe that everything in more expensive restaurants, which are not always crowded, is better and fresher. In any case, it is hypocritical to eat out so expensively and put spoiled salami on the bread at home. Not to mention the rest of the family, some of whom don't even have money for that, so selfish.

A new conflict was born immediately upon entering; it was clearly his intention to argue. When I refused, he started talking about connecting his gigantic cooler, asking if I had an extension cord.

I decided to opt for his dirty mess in the refrigerator.

The next day he threw it away himself, probably because he realized how dirty it actually looked, and it had already had an effect, possibly my sister had said something about it.

Some people like nothing more than to provoke conflict and cross boundaries, and he was undeniably one of them.

He had worn his pants at the campsite for two weeks without washing.

"Then now it's time for a clean one," I immediately thought when he said something about it.

"Not with dirty clothes on the clean couches here, it's not my chalet and the deposit is extremely high here!" That was also a sore leg, after some resistance and further insistence on my part, he agreed to it. .

They were given two bedrooms, it was clear that they were now only going to sleep together as husband and wife for form's sake, that normally mother/daughter - father/son was the usual combination, at least during holidays.

We assigned them the smallest bathroom, without a bath. They were clearly concerned about this and asked if they could share the bath with us, something we had very little interest in and did not do.

To my great surprise, after all this, the friend also started making a fuss about the euro tourist tax they had to pay for their free stay and it didn't stop there.

There was no question of strengthening family ties that was clear within an hour, in the days that followed I made the necessary effort, but whatever I did it was always wrong.

I thought it would be nice to meet up with family somewhere, to the great dissatisfaction of these and those, some of whom did their best to create a sense of solidarity, often in vain, or hypocritical relationships were developed that were ultimately aimed at financial gain, inheritances and the like.

The children were trained from an early age to ignore me and my eldest sister, at least we weren't called aunt, and everything had to change. The image they painted of us was very negative, wrongly so, especially in my case, I can only speak for myself in this matter.

In any case, what they were doing was very antisocial, the way they excluded people could almost be called fascist and underhanded, because behind your back they often talked about nothing else.

Sixty years of marriage to mom and dad

Along time later. Mom and Dad are sixty-year marriage was not much better, which is not surprising because there had been little contact in the intervening period. How a piece of meat can lead to a family feud!! Which was not my fault, I made endless attempts to talk things out, in vain, and it usually didn't go further than email contact. Once again a piece of meat was at stake, this time in a broader sense.

More than a year ago was their sixtieth wedding anniversary. I was not invited, but Richard was, even though he had already been paralyzed for a year, had been ill for seven years and now literally had nowhere to go. They supposedly didn't know that, almost none of my family, even though I had already told it a thousand times, so they did nothing to help. On the contrary, they told people everywhere that it was my fault, which made no sense at all. It was inhumanly difficult to have to take care of him alone, which I had to do largely alone for eight years, actually much longer. In his completely overstressed state and out of fear of death, he also occasionally showed a lot of aggression towards me.

I didn't have time for anything, every night I fell asleep exhausted, and there was a period when I hardly had any money for food, which they didn't care about and continued with all their parties and long journeys.

I found out about that invitation when I went to give them a gift the day before the party, apparently they felt guilty and I was invited after all. And I recently experienced it again when I received an invitation in the second term; I am the eldest of this family!

I struggled to find time the next day, which meant leaving Richard alone from around three in the afternoon until nine in the morning the next day, when he couldn't even get up from his makeshift bed in the house where he had to live for a while due to his illness. I had a lot of trouble, including arranging everything properly for him, but I did it anyway, dressed decently and went there on foot. When I arrived the group was already eating, it turned out that they had been partying all day! While I was invited to dinner, Dad, my stepfather, said I could come in for a moment. I almost died of hunger and after a year of eating carrots and potatoes I wanted to eat something different, it was very nice that someone cooked for me after all these years. My sister who had organized all this stood up from the table and said: "I'm not going to the table with that monstrosity!" I could have fallen through the floor but remained calm and said: 'I had counted on being able to eat with me, now I have to go get something from the freezer at home!'

I was allowed to sit at the table, but I didn't get anything to drink, at first, but eventually my friend got me a glass of water. It was terrible, I was attacked from all sides, including physically, the cutlery was literally pulled out of my hands, or at all actually. No one asked how Richard was doing (let alone me), which was the worst thing for me and I constantly wondered how it could be that people could be so heartless, people who actually have everything their heart desires.

I asked the question whether perhaps someone from the younger generation, people approaching ninety

Disclaimer

Although the information in this book has been compiled with great care, Carmen Barton accepts no liability for direct or indirect damage (of any nature) arising from or in any way related to this book, no rights can be derived from the content. derived. Statements are made based on Biblical knowledge, research and practical experience.

The author accepts no responsibility for organizations, companies and individuals referred to in this website.

Although this book may contain autobiographical elements, it should be seen as a form of fiction. Truths about certain topics can be explained from different points of view, and the diversity of points of view can illuminate many aspects of a given hypothesis.

Any form of use or distribution of posted articles in an offensive or discriminatory manner or with such an offensive purpose does not correspond to the objectives of Carmen Barton, is not legal, and is absolutely rejected by the creator, who cannot be held liable either. for events resulting from content in this book.